NATURAL HISTORY

NATURAL HISTORY

POEMS

BRANDON KILBOURNE

Winner of the Cave Canem Prize

Graywolf Press

Published by Graywolf Press
212 Third Avenue North, Suite 485
Minneapolis, Minnesota 55401

www.graywolfpress.org

Published in the United States of America

ISBN 978-1-64445-367-4 (paperback)
ISBN 978-1-64445-368-1 (ebook)

2 4 6 8 9 7 5 3 1
First Graywolf Printing, 2025

Library of Congress Cataloging-in-Publication Data

Names: Kilbourne, Brandon, 1983– author
Title: Natural history : poems / Brandon Kilbourne.
Description: Minneapolis, Minnesota : Graywolf Press, 2025.
Identifiers: LCCN 2025016372 (print) | LCCN 2025016373 (ebook) |
    ISBN 9781644453674 paperback | ISBN 9781644453681 epub
Subjects: LCSH: Natural history—Poetry | LCGFT: Poetry
Classification: LCC PS3611.I44958 N38 2025 (print) |
    LCC PS3611.I44958 (ebook) | DDC 811/.6—dc23/eng/20250422
LC record available at https://lccn.loc.gov/2025016372
LC ebook record available at https://lccn.loc.gov/2025016373

Cover design: Mary Austin Speaker

Cover photo: Courtesy of Brandon Kilbourne

For Emma

CONTENTS

III. DISPATCHES FROM ELLESMERE

IV. BLINDFOLD WONDER

FOREWORD

"Yet do I marvel at this curious thing . . ."

Reading Brandon Kilbourne's *Natural History*, I could not help thinking of Countee Cullen's poem, and of the marvel and curious things of this world on vivid display in this compelling debut collection. The opening section, titled "The Curious Institution," sets the tone, invoking a play on the history of "the peculiar institution" and its awful connection to natural history: the ships that carried an enslaved human cargo alongside plants, minerals, insects, all the specimens collected on exploratory journeys—the province of naturalists. Throughout the section, the poet places in juxtaposition the way that the pursuit of knowledge—what often begins in wonder—has been inextricably linked to greed, devastation both human and environmental, and destruction, as in these lines in the voice of an historical personae from the poem "Dioramic Idylls":

> Simply even to know
> this continent, bring
> its darkness under science's
> ken, a smear of blood
> sets in the creases of our palms.

Among the perspectives of explorers and scientists, visitors and guides of *Natural History* is that of the poet himself. As a research biologist working more than twenty years in natural history museums, Dr. Kilbourne has examined the artifacts and plumbed their meanings. The result is a complex meditation on wonder and devastation of the natural world and an elegy for the earth by an observer who sees, clear-eyed, the ways it "premonishes disappearance." Aptly, the wonder of the poet is likened to a marvelous universe wherein early trips to the American Museum of Natural History kindled the desire for scientific knowledge long before the understanding of its dark underbelly. The final poem, "Blindfold Wonder," finds the poet reflecting on the contradictions he's come to see clearly: his own place in the history of exploration and discovery ("I suppose that if Dr. Morton had met me, / he would have fantasized about my skull / assuming its place among the shelves / of his collection"); the "curated forgetting" and the "atrocities concealed / behind species christened out of Greek and Latin."

Reading these lines,

two decades later, no longer
prone to my boyhood's unseeing wonder,
I could read the symbols in the bronze sight
of Roosevelt greeting me at the museum's entrance,
his horseback height cementing his head far above
the paired African and American natives attending
him on foot . . .

I am reminded of my early love of books, forged in childhood: how they were to me then infallible repositories of knowledge before I came to understand the erasures and silences within them. Decades later, I encountered the hierarchies of race and difference codified by the great Enlightenment thinkers and philosophers and the way that my supposed place in the world was being constructed in those revered pages. Thomas Jefferson, writing—in *Notes on the State of Virginia* (1785)— "they have never yet been viewed by us as subjects of natural history," called for a kind of comparative anatomy, asserting that if scientists were to cut the negro open they would be able to ascertain the root of what he believed to be black inferiority. In those same pages, he declared: "Among the blacks is misery enough, God knows, but no poetry." Which is why I return to Countee Cullen. In "Yet Do I Marvel,"

Cullen slyly pushes back against that notion, calling to mind the many definitions of the word curious: not simply strange or novel, but made carefully—the precise handiwork of God, the necessity "To make a poet black, and bid him sing!" Kilbourne, too, pushes back against centuries of received knowledge, the carefully made "curious institution" of natural history and its concealments, the carefully made museum with its curated forgetting, silences, and erasures, even the scientists (then and now) who could never have imagined someone like him turning his early calling not only into scientific study but also into poetry. *Natural History* is a marvel.

Natasha Trethewey

NATURAL HISTORY

I. THE CURIOUS INSTITUTION

The Giraffe Titan (I)

*In the Museum für Naturkunde Berlin, the dinosaur exhibition is
composed largely of specimens excavated between 1906 and 1913
at Tendaguru, a site in the former colony of German East Africa
(today Tanzania). Of these dinosaurs, the most iconic is* Giraffatitan
brancai. *Coincidentally, European and other major world powers
met in Berlin, some twenty years prior to the dinosaurs' excavation,
at the Berlin Conference (1884–1885), where these powers negotiated
their claims to regions of Africa for colonial expansion.*

At the feet of a precipice-tall skeleton,
we wonder about the horrors of the Jurassic,
predators stalking, then slicing into, their prey.
Walking among Berlin's exhibited bones
embodying bridge-span necks and column
limbs, lance-point armor and knife-lined jaws,
we try to picture a world beyond our ken,
subject to claws evolved as killing
personified, laws of unremitting savagery—
Imagine on an over-muggy Earth, a head
towering above in the domain of treetops
and dogfighting pterosaurs, imagine
the head-crowned neck crashing down
like a felled alder, the impact thundering
as if a deposed god was hurled to Earth;
in final moments, would the aged Titan be able
to imagine scavengers biting into its cold skin,
its bones swallowed by tidal mud? Could
it then possibly imagine a world beyond its ken
hundreds of thousands of millennia later
in which twenty men in Berlin would carve
its continent into plantations, mines, and ivory-
hunting grounds, their talons manifest in
massacres charring within burning villages,

famine's gaunt ribs slowly quelling rebellions,
black skin in the mouths of ravenous empires?
Even if so, why try wondering at all?
A predator is a predator after all, regardless
of the time in Earth's history—they simply
differ in their habit and the hunt: some
sink their honed teeth into a scaly hide,
a roar professing their territory; others
convene over a landmass map, howling
false claims in English, French, and German.

Natural History, the Curious Institution

We do not often think of the wretched, miserable, and inhuman
spaces of slave ships as simultaneously being spaces of natural his-
tory. . . . The collections of these naturalists bear witness to the deeply
intertwined histories of the slave trade and early modern science in
the Atlantic.
> —Kathleen S. Murphy, "Collecting Slave Traders: James
> Petiver, Natural History, and the British Slave Trade"

Two months to the Caribbean,
our hold crammed tight
with cargo still breathing.

In Lisbon after eight weeks in the bowels
of a ship: samples of **CARMINE** and **INDIGO**,
preserved **SCALE INSECTS**, the dye's **DRIED FLOWER**.

FIFTEEN HUNDRED blocks iron ballast
to steady our galley with Negroes loaded, hull
plangent in rough seas' throes and tortures.

The right to sell slaves in New Spain accords
with our grand scheme—Imagine the returns
in American **HERBS**, the **CURES** and **REMEDIES**!

ELEVEN *of us tried to starve ourselves,*
but with a metal tool, the ship's surgeon prised
our mouths open, pouring gruel down our throats.

On picking up Jamaican **FISH** preserved in spirits, I met strident
abolitionists at the harbor. Yes, their treatment is abhorrent,
but a civilizing yoke can only be best for the African.

TWENTY percent of our Africans
written off to the squalor below deck:
diarrhea, fever, chains' wounds gangrened.

> Yesterday arrived a most diverse assortment of SEASHELLS
> in the hold of a new-built slaver; I detest the trade
> and pity their cargo, but science nonetheless must progress.

TWO HUNDRED AND TWELVE slaves salvaged
while rescuing people from our Guineaman
foundered amid reefs off the Swahili Coast.

> While leaving the Bight of Benin, a squall downed the ship
> fully loaded—truly a tragedy—the crew and captain lost
> along with specimens of RHINOCEROS, ANTELOPE, and BATS.

SIXTY-FOUR slaves staged a mutiny—We hailed
them with lead from our barricade, dispensing
viperous man, woman, and child overboard.

> En route to New Orleans, the slaves, I learned,
> mutinied, escaping to some small isle; with deepest
> displeasure I write that your MALACHITE nodules are lost.

THIRTY at a time they rowed us out to their great
and stinking ship, our bodies then chained
to planks stacked one atop another, coffin tight.

> Along with an array of DRIED LEAVES and SEEDS,
> my collector surprised me with a section of CARVED IVORY,
> showing the heathens' fancy and hand at detail.

FIVE HUNDRED AND TEN, we marched them down
to the shore; from the fort's white walls atop the hill,
the chaplain come down to bless our ship's sailing.

With the captain having lost on the journey only five
percent his Africans, and the safe arrival of these **NESTS**
and **EGGS**, we can both delight in a profitable enterprise.

A **DOZEN** jetsam corpses to bait the sharks—
We put on a show for the blacks, dissuading
any uprising with the terror of bloodied waves.

Enclosed is an enormous **SNAKE** from Suriname: a gentleman
by the name of De Jong generously loaned me a troop
of his blacks to procure the beast and prepare its **SKELETON**.

*THREE HUNDRED AND ONE of our number passing on
with no return; in subsequent weeks' chains,
the iron savored our blood and entered our souls.*

Upon stowing the chains for those wretches, fill
the hold with the sugar, rum, and cotton, and find some
room for these crates, **BONES** for some naturalist in Paris.

FORTY lashes to stripe the back of that nigger
flashing a bold eye: we'll not have him abuse
our kind ration of sun and air above deck.

Six **SPECIES** named in the last years, all received
through the safe care of the forts and their garrisons
that stock ships calling along the Slave Coast.

ONE African wench brained
dead amid the crew's night whoring: £30
her price docked from their wages.

The accounts of **HARPY VULTURE** and **SLOTH** are remarkable,
but the loathsome vessel for this knowledge bottoms on
the question: are our morals to be the price of discovery?

ONE HUNDRED AND THIRTY-TWO sick and infirm
the defendants pitched to the waves; dire
straits did not impel them, but rather insurance.

Five skins of fabulous PURPLE FEATHERS—Having delivered
your slaves to port, I trust bringing these and other
articles back to Liverpool shall not burden you.

Two minds broken, one left, one right of me,
their every breath a wail in the ship's dark, where
vermin nipped and crawled over our shackled bodies.

A simply unacceptable matter—Fifty percent
the BUTTERFLIES gnawed down to tatters, no doubt
from the vermin and filth housed in that ship's belly.

THREE children—Nos. 8, 19, 46—we put
into the thumbscrews, to force the betrayal
of the Negroes that led the quelled revolt.

Just this week, I catalogued my latest curiosities—
CRABS and CORALS brought by the *Navigator*
from Barbados, vibrant in their colors.

THREE THOUSAND miles between Whydah
and Salvador, COUNTLESS the ocean's
tears purling back to homelands severed.

Having the captain as my guest over dinner, I extolled
to him his role in advancing NATURAL HISTORY—
To our benefit, his contributions number COUNTLESS.

Dioramic Idylls

I.

Building dioramas
rigid and resonant,
deft hands stage untouched
wildernesses like requiems
for guttering species:

returning from the bamboo understory, the red
panda balancing on a thinning branch of canopy.

Following the riverbank below the escarpment,
three takins navigating Bhutanese mists.

These facsimiles of living
anatomies motionlessly evoke
a nature unscathed
in our visitor eyes—

Swept by the museum's alcoves
enclosing carefully arrayed wax
leaves, croppings of mangals, gleanings
of cloud forests, mounted skins
of floe-berthed walrus and scree-denned pika,
we press a relic
dream upon animal faces:
pockets of Earth escaped
intact, harmony rippling
from advancing girders and asphalt,
vanguard clearings for farmland.

Hermetic behind their glass pane,
the addaxes we find exotic, their coats
candent against Libya's red sands.

Yet we know innately
the ecology of vultures:

a zebra's rigored limb jutting
from their throng, their raised wings
veil their gore-riddled beaks.

The hyenas stalk their frenzy.

II.

October 17th 1912
Faradje, Belgian Congo

We negotiated the ransacking's trails—
the train bypassing rock-thrash
rapids, the small stations stringing
coastal Boma to Stanley Pool;
the steamboat chugging the horizon-
flood river, anchoring evening
explorations en route to Stanleyville;
the seven-month trudge alongside porting
shoulders, the file of black torsos made
packhorses to bring us to far-off Faradje.
Availing ourselves to inroads for felled ivory,
we skirted like puddles yesterday's
blood wrung out by charnel rubber:

    Bodies peeled to sap and bone,
    the numberless number:

        hands littering the dirt like
        bullet casings, stumps

            shrieking for fingers
            and palms piled in baskets—

    Bodies flayed to sap and bone,
    the numberless number:

        bloodletting vines of *chicotte*, iron
        vines dangling from neck

to neck, flesh devoured
by civilizing cannibals—

Bodies flensed to sap and bone,
the numberless number: colony's agar.

Coffers and cargo holds brimming
demand a wilderness reduced
to piano keys, chess pieces, ink pad
stamps, figurines of saints, trophies,
erasers, tires, hoses, gaskets,
stoppers for bottles, ornate inlays,
curios from a romanticized continent.
We stampede horns and claws,
tusks and pelts to the perished
menagerie of quagga and bluebuck,
passenger pigeon and great auk—

Simply even to know
this continent, bring
its darkness under science's
ken, a smear of blood
sets in the creases of our palms.

⌁

In the kerosene's sallow light,
rain thundering upon our tent sprawl,
the day's achievement eyeless
stares back at me:
our third and final example
of the northern white rhinoceros,
its hide salted and drying beside

bundles of tall grass, rolls of
undeveloped film, and collected insects
that shrink a habitat down to an alcove.

I've always been more comfortable
behind the camera than
behind the rifle's sights.
Photographing one of our hunters
proudly posing beside the hulking
carcass, I can't help but
feel the architect
of death, yet
I know the photo
of a mountain of bison
skulls—the buffalo skinner standing
on its summit, boasting
from its bone-stacked height
of our natural talent—

Cuvier only deduced extinction
in 1796. In little more than a century,
we have already mastered it.

III.

The snatchings pane-sealed
of Congolese rainforests, Kenai taiga,
Iguaçú cataracts, Namib dunes and
outcrops transport us. Carcasses
hand-arranged from field notes resurrect
the world without handprint smokestacks,
usurping pasture, knots of highway,
pretend we haven't devoured the Earth,
leaving our eyes to probe their glass
eyes. Their thick skins' presence
dissolves the distance,
anchors in the firsthand fauna
of photographs and nature films—
This herd of elephants in low light,
admiring their wrinkled trunks, tapered
ivory, we forget that we march them
dwindling to join sea cows, sea mink,
the hapless dodo.

IV.

The origin of the wolverine:

> My idling taillights color the roadside snow,
> highlight its fur with embers' red.
>
> The clouds sift their burial of stocky limbs
> returned to a habitat fragmented
>
> by macadam, logging saws, and summer cabins.
> Here, where once they ranged southerly, bereft
>
> of their footprints, the snows speak
> their elegy. I gauge its body half-
>
> frozen—the skull crushed, but the skin
> without puncture, specimen-worthy.
>
> A truck passing in bluster
> of motor and exhaust outpaces
>
> adaptation, reveals evolution's
> lacking foresight: Pleistocene-honed
>
> snowshoe paws, shear-edge carnassials
> are useless in the advent of crankshaft speed,
>
> headlights overwhelming retinas.
> With late remorse of the prodigal
>
> species, I salvage the body, belly setting
> with ice, and place it in the trunk of my car.

V.

We can only achieve the dead harmony—

    Cloud banks storm-tinged, malachite
    canopies lie in the background's oils
    above a swath of ochre brushstrokes melting
    into Uele tallgrass ringing the foreground;

        at its center

      a small wallowing hole,

  to its left

  scales stretched over a body shaped
  from twine and wood-wool,

          to its right

    three hides fitted over plaster cast sculptures,
        long horns capping their snouts—

    the small pangolin and the crash of rhinos
    posed in still standoff awkward,
    drama of armor and lances.

    Behind their glass exists no desire
    for false cures of ground horns and scales.

The meticulous details overawe us:
two leaning egrets lost in the wallow's

engineered reflection.

VI.

Boreal vestige: atop its bluff, the lone
wolverine surveys the cratonic vista,
sparse trees and the grays of extinct
volcanoes splayed to the horizon—
The rose of twilight culminates
in the air, the haze as pristine
as one perfected only in frescoes.

They comfort the return visitor—
These habitats that never change:
idylls for the wrecked earth.

Rhinoceros Relic

On a diorama of the Sumatran rhinoceros (Dicerorhinus sumatrensis)
at the former Copenhagen Zoological Museum. Critically endangered,
the total population for the species is estimated at fewer than eighty,
and possibly as few as thirty, individuals.

In the guise of sunlight breaking
through a canopy of wax leaves,
a patch of lamplight salvages
the forequarter robust as a column
from a body dissolved in darkness,
attesting that they once lumbered
outside of memory's borders
between first charging out of the Miocene
and vanishing into diorama shadows—

    Panzer-hide shoulder
    the neck downward sloping
    to a wood-burl eye.

Born of mud wallows, lianas, and mists,
a skin preserves the extant likeness
of an intended mother taken as air cargo
crated crampedly to Copenhagen's gray
concrete, metal bars, and heating
on the gamble her newborns would ensure
that those mud wallows, lianas, and mist-
slicked thickets would always harbor
fresh tracks bearing three broad toes—

    Paired and namesake
    horns borne atop a head, low
    barrows stricken with myth.

The zoo's dead captive imitates
its life in a locale of faux mud fitted
with kingfishers, stick insects,
and stalks of bamboo, their display
an elegy in gloom—glass eyes cry
pristine boles falling before plantations
and habitats invaded by logging trucks,
faces clear-cut to oblivion
by our keratinous greed—

    Rainforest behemoth, relict
    red hair recalling woolly kin
    grazing on Ice Age steppes.

Behind an exhibit's pane, taxidermied
feet fill the footprints of a lost species,
leaving a mounted remembrance
tangible for its final refuge: our fantasy
where wild animals live on and still exist
with nostrils estranged from their breath,
bodies stiff bereft of the faintest twitch,
and no note of bird trill is to be heard
in a glassed-in jungle's cemetery silence.

    Shrine to an extinction's skin, beast
    shepherded to the fabled ranks of a ram
    golden fleeced—priceless once flayed.

The Last Sea Cow's Testimony

Steller's sea cow (Hydrodamalis gigas) *first encountered Europeans in 1741 after the shipwreck of the* St. Peter *on Bering Island during the Great Northern Expedition. Within twenty-seven years of its first contact with Europeans, the sea cow was hunted to extinction.*

Fittingly, the first of them arrived
in disaster, as, like a whirlpool,
only disaster spirals about them—

As dawn gilded the bay after a night
of squall-stoked swells, we beheld them like
a haggard omen visited upon us by the tide:

not a single cow, otter, or seal could remain
incurious of the whale-sized driftwood
that they rode here wind-quickened

atop the waves, but before long
we grasped that they know only to flout
their anatomy's boundaries, for how else

could they dare the ocean to reach these floes
and snowy sands, and, plainly lacking flukes
or fins to scull home, strand themselves here?

Granted, they are resourceful, to and fro
the shore scouring for driftwood, from which,
somehow, they sparked light and warmth;

nonetheless, their frailty abounds—
From the shallows, we could watch their skin
blue from damp and blizzard, spy how

their number thinned, gaunt and stiff limbs
piled over with sand, how their sick laid prone
to the nibbling teeth of foxes. Yet

never in the maw of an orca devouring a calf,
neither in the eyes of a cormorant, gullet full of fish,
nor in the face of an otter flecked with urchin

had we witnessed anything like their habitual
barbarity—I remember watching cows dragged
and beached on shore, their bodies methodically

butchered to the bone, my mate's skin torn off
as she writhed her tail, the twin spurts erupting
from her opened back with each dying gasp,

my sight stained red as her life gushed out
into the water, and, as they took her apart,
their blood-splattered ardor—This slaughter

finding us nearly thirty winters ago, back when
every cow, otter, and seal had to learn survivor's
wisdom: trade your curiosity for fear.

After they devised their escape from the island,
we thought that we could reclaim our peace,
returning to the lives we had before they came,

relish unbothered the last of the summer kelp,
the sea rocking us, bellies filled, to sleep,
sun glints skittering wave to wave after days of fog,

until again, wind at their tail, they dotted the offing,
our dwindled herds yet dwindling as more and more
they arrived to haul us life-robbed from the water.

Now I am the last of the sea cows, my heart's
continued beating, my tail's propelling labor,
my streamlined existence all become hopeless

defiance of our disappearance. Departing seaward
into a sapphire void, I speak a vanishing tongue
now no one else understands to spite the silence

closing over us forever, entrusting this account
to my bones that will litter the seafloor, my eye sockets
soon home to crabs who will never glimpse a sea cow.

Lettow-Vorbeck and His Uncatchable Lizard

Shortly after World War I, the dinosaur Dysalotosaurus
lettowvorbecki *was named for the German general Paul von
Lettow-Vorbeck for his defiance of Allied forces in East Africa
during the war. The dinosaur's Greek-derived name means
"Lettow-Vorbeck's uncatchable lizard."*

A dinosaur christened in honor of your valiant service:
an uncatchable lizard for the uncatchable general.

Epochs upon epochs before becoming *der Löwe
von Afrika* for your wartime exploits of raiding and
evasion that drove the British to pursue in vain
your lone and vastly outmanned *Schutztruppe*
across savannah and forest for four man-killing years,
your dinosaur relied on fleet limbs to escape the jaws
of Jurassic predators in the land you would later
defend as *Deutsch-Ostafrika* with forces dwindling.

Its long tail would counterbalance the body nimble
on two legs as your beast darted about to fulfill
its niche of munching on leaves—the small head
and tiny hands, the peg teeth woefully antithetical
to the arts of aggression perhaps leaving your namesake
as something of a letdown and you a misnomer
for a creature so ill-equipped for devouring valor—

With locusts' unsparing hunger, you and your askaris
wantonly consumed fields and livestock, relieving
food from the mouths it was reared to feed, giving
in return calamity to land-grab colonies: mass famine
to fuel European shells falling on African soil,
boneyards sprung from villages starved and skeletons
by the multitude marking routes trod by your troops.

But after seeing the bone-lean bodies trailed behind
your soldiers' growling stomachs, the unearthing
of your uncatchable lizard would have offered you
a sight recognizable though rewritten in rock: mass death
albeit fossilized as ribs and femora, vertebrae and maxillae
jumbled in the thousands, remains of tide-drowned
herds befitting the toll of your disaster, the bellies
without number that you condemned to die empty.

To your name, your dinosaur brings an exhumed honor:
its bones bestowing on you the renown of a mass grave.

The Giraffe Titan (II)

*With a long upright neck and forelimbs longer than hindlimbs,
the sauropod dinosaur* Giraffatitan brancai *bore a superficial
resemblance to a titanic giraffe, with this similarity serving as
inspiration for its name.*

Here in Berlin from Africa,
taken from Tendaguru's hills!

Lofty among the atrium's
glass and steelwork high overhead,

eye-socketed summit of bone—
the Giraffe Titan, astride Earth

once again! Do not strain your necks
as you gaze upward in awe, dwarfed

by Mesozoic proportions—
Depleting a continent green,

between this cavernous ribcage
and pelvis sat the source of its

insatiable appetite that
was fed by devouring its way

across Africa's rife lushness.
Strung along these gargantuan

bones were insensate muscles, their
violent contractions swinging

the limbs lumbering wantonly
to leafy troves snatched by its maw.

Next, note how the skull would look out
from this neck tall as a tree's trunk,

the inhuman height distancing
higher thoughts from the disasters

waged as each footfall would convulse
the earth, the trail of footprint scars.

Do grasp, ladies and gentlemen,
that before you stands the terror

of its time, hunger incarnate
covered in scales, a creature who,

by a glutton's nature, would not
leave a single leaf on a twig

as whole forests suffered its teeth,
entire lakes flowing as rivers

guzzled down a sluice-long throat,
vast wilds fouled to wastes by sludge dung.

My good people, I implore you
to know that this scourge preyed upon

lands home to other animals,
availing itself to the food

that would sustain them, untroubled
by whether then they might perish.

Woeful species that could not flee
were left to the famines sprouting

from its presence, fields of ribs bleached
by the sun, with any challenge

extinguished by the immense weight
crushing bodies beneath four feet.

Be thankful that our Berlin Beast
is but a nightmare's memory

bound to this defunct skeleton—
Please, though, take care to remember:

evolution has a knack for
repetition, reinventing

wings among birds, bats, and beetles,
sleek fins among sharks and dolphins—

She's likewise over the ages
rehashed her ravaging Titan,

finding a new form to harbor
its continent-gorging greed.

From Europe's soil, her behemoth's
avarice arose once again,

albeit in a much smaller
human's stature. Staking feeding

grounds in Africa through charnel
colonies, this voracity

without end tried in vain to cram
itself full, stuffing its mouth with

diamonds and sapphires, rubber's sap,
gold and copper, clear-cut timber,

medicinal herbs, ivory
and hides, animals bound for zoos,

fossils destined for museums,
plantation-grown cocoa and cane,

coffee, sisal, and palm's red oil,
despoiled rivers and vistas, lands

fertile, grasses for cattle, men
yoked faceless for brute hard labor.

If you were to tremble at just
the mention of such crazed desire

not content until Africa
was consumed down to mere pebbles,

I could not blame you. However,
do know I tell you these horrors

alongside the bones showcased here
so you can recognize as truth

that sheer rapacity apt for
a dinosaur can masquerade

as something human, giving you
no future reason to gawk, breath

stoppered by a gasp betraying
an ignorance of our darkest

nature. Take this chance to acquaint
yourselves with this recurring bane

so to know when it walks the Earth
again, as we can but surely

wager that this monstrosity
will be reborn at a mere whiff

of wealth wafting from soil, luckless
lands left to fend off famished jaws.

II. MEMORY MUSEUM

Memory Museum

At the Museum für Naturkunde Berlin

Among chalk-white, tallowed, and war-sooted
bones, upstairs away from the tourists and gaggles
of kindergartners, we discussed the slow arc
of evolution in the hours of that afternoon.
I disinterred the dead from their cardboard
boxes and cabinet sepulchres, placing before you
a pangolin's toothless skull, scraps of dried baleen,
the spiraled lance of a narwhal—memories
of scourged termites and African savannahs,
hooves become flippers and mouthfuls of krill,
ocean migrations and Greenland's ice floes
lighting curiosity's wick in your eyes.
I remember seeing for the first time the fox
tessellated in ink that you smuggle between
your shoulder blades, your coat draped over arm
as we earlier walked an edifice, itself a memory
of colony and war, a divvied city, and a mother
bringing her toddler to see dinosaurs—the Earth's own
stone memory—though you said that you were too young
to recall. Returning downstairs from aardwolves
and crabeater seals, strolling among pedestaled
planets, you recited the old mnemonic *Mein Vater
Erklärt Mir Jeden Sonntag Unsere Neun Planeten*
to knead more German into my tongue before
we saw perched as still life a memory Himalayan:
red fur dangling its tail's fulvous rings. Fulgurous,
an arc raced from cheeks to shoulder
to your raised arm and the stone-rigid
fingertip firing *Red panda!* off your tongue—
a three-syllable echo of Bang immemorial.

The Origami Fox

It was to be a singular effort—
Will bounding from rustling undergrowth
tangled across the heart's shadowy floor
to cast away its shyness and join Skill,
ventured from its den at the back of a brain.
And so impetus and expertise frolicked
in sweat wrung from a knotted brow bent
upon a symbol to shoulder timorous words:
thick orange paper joining soft white tissue
in perfect square, receiving crease upon
crease in stepping-stone folds, taking shape
over patient and deliberate hours, gaining
a sturdy spine, a bushy tail, and four legs first crude
then svelte, all adorned in a color-change coat,
till at last care-weary fingers formed ears,
a nose, and a tapered snout with snowy cheeks.
With dabbed water, life was contoured
into a paper fox enfolding a foothold
to a heart. Borne by their vulpine labor,
Will and Skill basked in the dazzle
of azure irises ablaze with a smile,
forerunners of the fox-maker's long-desired
kiss. And in love's heedless bliss, blue and brown
eyes lost themselves in the other pair's spell, spurring
fingers to clasp two hands together, palm to palm.
Thinking they had predestined a fairy-tale
future, Will and Skill retired to their dens
at the root of a heart and the back of a brain, yet
what was a happy tale shortly corroded to naught,
and glints between eyes brown and blue became spent,
as words silk soft gained glass's broken edge,
as smiles ever feebler collapsed under their own weight,
as laughter's clapper grew heavier till it stilled,

as true faces emerged from behind cracked masks,
and kindness foundered in a gulf's silence.
And in attic aftermath of blue and brown eyes parting,
housed in a box streaked with dusty daylight,
the paper fox heartless, the paper fox brainless,
the paper fox aired in the absence of any ears,
What did he expect folded paper to know
about destiny's chances and storybook bliss?
And the paper fox settled into its slumber
in the cardboard's closed-box darkness.

Boyhood's Fields

Those fields were totally empty to me,
though in your universe, their tilled earth was where,
like a seedling, boyhood was reared for manhood.
Driving for aimless hours the back roads connecting
Duson, Breaux Bridge, and other small towns,
taking the most circuitous route possible to tour
the dealerships and view their newest tractors,
we would first visit the comic book store,
your five-minute concession for monthly
adventures of Darkhawk and Venom.

Those fields, though, stayed empty to me,
so you would point out your universe—
Look at the cows! Look at the corn!
—your finger's thrust bringing into existence
the ilk of alfalfa, John Deere, sugarcane, and combines,
turkeys and deer opportunely in the open,
and everyday chevrons of geese gliding overhead,
while I preferred the inhabitants of the Marvel Universe—
thumbing through trading cards of Rhino, Stegron, and She-Hulk—
as daydreams of *Tyrannosaurus* roared from the Cretaceous.

And those fields remained empty to me, so you
once more pressed your universe upon me—
Look at the geese! Look at the geese!
—before seeding me in my boredom with salted words—
Nigger, would you wake your ass up? You're in
for a rude awakening! A rude awakening!
—as we drove down a road like a fault line
dividing small family farms and their differing crops.
And so those fields remain empty to me, their furrows forever
blighted by the mouthfuls of salt you sowed among their soil.

Noriko

A waitress, her figure hazy save for
the bob and sweep of a black ponytail,

wide cheekbones dimpled with laughter
lingering for decades somehow unblurred,

a voice now a memory having no longer
a word, a leftover husk of timbre and accent.

Yet her fading belies the recollection—
Respites under warm restaurant lights,

makeshift kith eclipsing insular couples,
the weeks' bevies of closed Denverites

abated over morsels of yellowtail and crab.
Accompanying each meal, small lessons

snuck in between ferrying *donburi*
to tables and jotting down orders

—schooling me in traditional breakfasts, a free
bowl of *negi*-topped tofu, its cube overly soft—

or during closing, in the quiet slowness
of the last customers finishing their beers

—huddled over a menu, *sakana* (魚) the choice
to demystify for me the reading of kanji.

The amiable gravity of a smile, its pull helping
a newcomer to find sure footing on the Earth.

Simple kindnesses become a three-month staple:
mainstay of that first summer alone in a city.

Stopgap fondness sunk down in a name, retrieved
to the surface when sounding three syllables.

Orison

She braids a rope from her fresh wound,
she braids three strands, she speaks three words.
Lord have mercy. Lord have mercy.
Long skeins are prayed from her soul's heart
for ropewalks stretching from a wound
to her tongue's tip. Within her words
creaks a taut rope tethered to shade
and solace beneath His aegis.

Lord have mercy. Lord have mercy.

Bloodied by fall onto cobbles,
my mother's mouth weaves a three-strand rope
as she sits under fluorescents.
Lord have mercy. Lord have mercy.
An unfaltering tongue pulls taut
a deliverance graspable,
her creaking orisons sounding
sure salvation under His shield.

Lord have mercy. Lord have mercy.

From her fresh wound she braids three strands,
she speaks three words, she braids a rope.
Lord have mercy. Lord have mercy.
Long skeins plaited in a ropewalk,
her orisons strain bolts in locks
of empyreal gates, her words
imploring after the promise
of succor beneath His aegis.

Lord have mercy. Lord have mercy.

She braids three words from her fresh wound
under emergency room lights,
draws taut a lifeline of three strands.
Lord have mercy. Lord have mercy.
Awaiting the doctor's return
with her jaw's X-ray, she nurses
her gash with talisman-tone words,
tending herself under His shield.

Mercy, may her Lord have mercy.

Weight belied by weightless plaitings
sounds solid a rope from her soul's
heart in revelation aural:
three words straining heaven's gates.

Frau Kahnt

Again her voice aged soft tries out
my ears, hopeful for a breakthrough
while I open a can too much
for her arthritis; neighborly,
her syllables don't shy away
from my scant vocabulary
as she copes with loss leaving her
marooned in her ninety-two years.

Hearing me out in the hallway,
she tethers greetings to old books,
fresh strawberries, and birthday cake,
only to watch sound German words
founder as emptied sounds butting
an English impasse—Supplanting
language, a rust-shut penknife speaks
fluent goodwill, leaving her hands.

❧

I listen to your eyes plangent,
your voice blind in my feckless ears—
Witness imprisoned in your tongue
withers to sparsely strung atoms:
U-Boot. Bomben. Dresden. Mutter.
Mein Mann ist tot seit acht Jahren.
Trembling eyes crave life for the dead
in graves sealed by my poor German.

❧

Undeterred, she ventures outside
zeitgeists frozen in furniture,

photos' inhabitants, knickknacks
gilded with memories, her steps
retreading the path to my door:
with a doorbell's press, her finger
translates beyond all words spoken
the loneness shawling her shoulders.

Otepää Snowscape

On the bus from Tartu, in a silence inviting
only whispers, I asked you of the word
vangla—crowned by a golden lion, its white parking lot
between the highway's traffic and its razor wire
nearly empty—when I was dumbstruck
at a bead of eyeliner leaving your eye,
as if your face could need any makeup.
Setting out upon arriving in Otepää,
you toured me through the winter capital,
wending us left and right, *vasakale*
and *paremale* aiming your pointing finger
as we walked lanes stitching together
dormant cars, footpaths and benches,
tiered pines and barren alders, staid
storefronts into a small town transmuted
picturesque by snow. Finding warmth withdrawn
into windows, lazily drifting upwards
from chimneys, I spurred myself on
with furtive glimpses of your eyes
kaleidoscopic with greens afield gray, even
as the gelid air plied knives at our canthi,
and my shoes ill-suited to your jaunt
laid me on slicked snow at your feet.
Standing at the closed doors of Maarja's Church,
I listened to you tell me of your tricolor—
sini-must-valge—its bronzed story flanking the doors.
Drifting to the low stones of the churchyard wall,
beneath a long branch alabaster with the season,
we seemed to enjoy our silence, which you later
called *vaikus*, as we looked across at a hill,
its castle's ruins covered by clouds' dreamy siftings,
the hillward snows stretching before us, stark
and pristine as a prison in winter.

It Came from Beneath the Sea

In the Mercadão São Paulo

I only came upon this small sea monster
after following by nose a whiff of salt
tinging the air as I toured among vibrant
baggies of *urucum* and turmeric, *carne seca*
weighed and priced by the gram, wending
until I was enveloped by the brine odor
emanating from the market's fishmongers,
the Portuguese labels among the morning's
catch—*namorado, corvina, robalo*—
making mysteries out of the buffed-coin
eyes and silver sheen scales laid out on ice.

But I only glimpsed the shelled oddity now
in my hand after walking over to view
the goopy flowers of overturned octopuses,
dark beaks at the center of suckered petals,
when three chitinous tanks arrested
my attention: their pebbly brown carapaces
each inset with a pair of sighted black pearls,
while, most strange, two shovels jutted
from their faces, crafted out of flat plates.
According to their display label, I was
gawking at *cavaquinha*, the Portuguese term,
I guess, for a lobster adapted to look absurd.

Amused that my discovery of a shellfish
would leave me so visibly transfixed,
especially since in all likelihood
this is a creature that he commonly sells,
one of the fishmongers stopped replenishing
his counter's crushed ice to reach me

a *cavaquinha*, letting me inspect leisurely
and up close its heavy armor coupled
with a complete lack of pincers, ten legs
spindly and claw tipped, the jointed plates
protruding as spades from its head.

As I pore over the animal in my hand,
I flash back to my childhood home's garage,
where my dad's co-workers would drop off
ice chests chock-full of fresh seafood.
No older than a preschooler, I remember
raptly watching my dad's large hands
fish through ice cubes to point out
the flat, asymmetrical faces of flounders,
the swimmerets of shrimp, and, above all
the pallid bodies of squid, black spotted
and limp tentacled, taking care to show me
in the light of the raised door the tiny
teeth ringing their suction cups—
an introductory lesson in marine zoology
which later led me to sit mesmerized
by the black-and-white mayhem of
It Came from Beneath the Sea, in which
a colossal octopus in stop-motion wrath
hauls itself out of the water to crumple
the Golden Gate Bridge, flamethrowers
eventually repelling eight arms back
into San Francisco Bay, their radioactive
rampage brought to a halt on our TV.

I return the *cavaquinha* to the fishmonger,
grateful for goodwill toward my curiosity.
As the crustacean passes between us,
we trade smiles in lieu of any word outside
obrigado—thanks given in Portuguese

for again learning that I share the Earth
with animals beyond my imagination,
the lobster glimpsed behind a fish counter
just the same as a squid held in the sun
of an open garage door. Perhaps they lack
the spectacle of B movie sea monsters
writhing boneless limbs to crush police
cars and pull apart clock towers, but
their bodies plucked from the sea to grace
dinner plates offer a marine reminder
that even the most fantastic wonder
may be little more than hunger's bycatch.

Moqueca Chronicle

Having traveled with me to Berlin
from a bookstore in São Paulo
after a first taste in Belo Horizonte,
a concoction of fish and coconut milk:
gram measures of chili and ginger each
have a turn on the cutting board
where my hands ply the blade,
while dried shrimp and peppercorns,
coriander seeds and turmeric
await them in the mortar—
small and flavorful morsels
recounting ancestral homelands,
origins and destinations retraced
with the ink of a recipe's ingredients.

With the tilt of a measuring spoon,
I drizzle a vermeil ribbon of oil
to smooth the pestle's grindings,
a scant teaspoon of Atlantic Africa
carried across ocean in casks stashed
in belowdecks' fetid and coffin dark,
stirred into horsebeans and dab-a-dab
passed out in crews to manacled hands,
smeared over wounds masked with caustic
ten days out from the Bay of All Saints,
rubbed over irons' and the cat's
scars to boost the price of black skin,
off-loaded along the coast of Bahia, where
amidst transplant groves of *dendê* and coconut,
firelight licking chains and window bars,
it sizzled in a *senzala*'s cooking pot.

A bit of oil collected under my nails
marks my touch yellow as I mix salt

and a lime's juice with soft cubes
of wels, white fish work-around
for Berlin's lack of Brazilian fish.
Two handfuls of crawfish tails throw in
a touch of my birthland, recalling shells
boiled red and dumped across newsprint,
schoolyard discoveries of mud chimneys
constructed overnight by industrious claws.

The oil's red fragrance wafts over
from dicings of tomatoes and onions,
mortar-made paste, chili and garlic all vocal
from the stove's eye—I pour into the pan
a liter of coconut milk, small lake wandered
with Portuguese profiteers and spice seekers
on carrack and caravel from Indian beaches,
finding root along the Gulf of Guinea to join
the company of rice, cowpeas, and okra, before
continuing along routes of Brazil-bound slavers
to commingle with annatto, cashews, and cassava,
where centuries after this journey,
setting out through cookbook pages,
it gains a foothold in my kitchen.

After so many times cooking this dish,
I can recite its preparation in full; now
I annotate the steps recorded in a single page,
its succinct ink belying circuitous creation,
to pinpoint my own touches in the margins.
Manning a spoon, I watch the turmeric
marble the coconut's white with yellow,
each circle of my hand further conjuring a hue
from monks' robes to overtake the pan, its
full brilliance coaxed out with a simmer.

Bringing the pan to a greater boil, I add the fish
to the vibrant and sputtering cacophony,
the melding cauldron redolent with Worlds
Old and New, spice caravans of the Silk Road
and Sahel, the aftermath of the Crusades, ambitions
of empires, conquistadors and the conquered,
unknown sails and unnamed lands dotting
horizons, saffron fortunes, food offerings
to orishas. Deeper than all this, like an anchor
down at the bottom of this thickening sauce,
the delight of tasting and embracing new flavors:
attested to by a tourist's first ignorant bite
on a rainy August night in Belo Horizonte.

To finish, I toss in red and green rings
of bell peppers, wedges of onions and tomatoes,
and, after a few minutes cooking, dust the stew's
yellow with green handfuls of scallion and cilantro,
richen its taste with two red tablespoons of oil.
I spoon the *moqueca* over rice, and my plate holds
an heirloom from a continent estranged,
recovered, despite history's capsizing swells,
through a fork's tines. Dispersing birthright
of diasporal millions arrived and born
in a forced homeland, the *dendê* and coconut
I savor and share, their scent filling my home
as they continue their odyssey carried by the full
stomachs departing my apartment at evening's end,
each dinner a miniscule and fundamental
footnote feeding their oceanic chronicle.

Erinnerung

On those white sands, we inhabit
the word that you taught me,
dotting the quilt of sunbathers,
the kiteboarders' turquoise playground
glistered to the offing.
Self-conscious of the found
beauty raying out in the thin
lines etching your cheeks and temples,
I instead stare down at your naked legs,
your toes dug into the sand.
Watching the kite-towed boards rollick
under the cloud-free blue, we practice each
other's mother tongue, haltingly
recounting kindred gray childhoods,
one where the father is
unloving and cold,
die andere wo der Vater
herrisch und kontrollsüchtig ist.
Translating my boyhood back to English,
you say, *Your father is*
a coward, as I listen with my eyes
upon your hands worked rough,
your lava-blond hair spilled down your neck.
On those white sands, we inhabit
the word that you that afternoon taught me,
Erinnerung—the name of a small isle
standstill with turquoise and sunlight's blue,
where two strangers speak two languages while
kites zip over combers in midday's hours—
a timeless island that outlives
its own sinking beneath the waves,
indelible as scars speaking
of paternal wounds.

Creation Myth

Spiraling headlong in each other's gravity,
we plucked loose strands of creation
for the fuse to wind around our binary orbit—

From among a trove of fish prototyped
fin upon spine in barren niches, anatomies
radiating in light-starved depths.

From clods of pure iridium and iron
crater-smelted from meteorites, atoms
smithed in sidereal meltdowns.

From stone feathers splayed around
bones of birds' newfound wings, petals
gathered for a gorgon's pressed rose.

From the Mesozoic's monsters rescued
from chthonic strata, vertebrae
stacked to breach the empyrean.

From among a red panda's hairs, a flint
to strike against your eye's umber, spark
kindling silver-glimmer constellations.

Curating the debris of spent epochs,
we ignited our inaudible bang, genesis
with the thunder of butterfly wingbeats—

Pair nebulous in the primordial bliss,
we firm our bodies with a deifying flame, two
wreathing coronae, overbright and dissembling.

III. DISPATCHES FROM ELLESMERE

Found on Ellesmere Island, the 375-million-year-old fossil *Tiktaalik roseae* was a fish that possessed a functioning wrist, which constituted an important step in the evolution of limbs from fins and the first expansion of vertebrates onto land from water. *Tiktaalik's* wrist indicates that it was likely an ancestor to the more than 30,000 species of amphibians, reptiles, birds, and mammals living today. In June 2006, an expedition was launched to Ellesmere Island, of which I was part, to recover new specimens of *Tiktaalik* along with other fish from the Devonian Period.

The Location We Look For

Arriving on Ellesmere Island

With the killing of the propellers' spinning,
we disembark to the sound of the Twin
Otter's engines cooling off, metal ticking
from heat lost to the Arctic's cold.
So the pilot can get on with his return
to Resolute, we empty the plane's
red-and-white body of our gear, piling on
the shore the plaster, the chisels and mauls,
tents, glue, brushes and awls, eight
sleeping bags and rucksacks, a jackhammer
and shovels, plus hand lenses, along
with a stove and the month's supply of food.

As our ride shrinks to a speck, the drone
of its propellers thinning into silence,
we survey the shore, our eyes seeing nothing
but ice's white, mud's brown, and the blues
of languorous waves and cloudless skies,
the seashore's wash and swatches of slush
embellished with unimpeded sunlight.

But we have not come for this place.
The location we look for lies underground,
now a memory repressed down in rock
recalling this island before it was even
an island, where a fish and its near kin
tinkered with fins to bear a body's weight
and free themselves from water, back when
this land beneath our feet sat at the equator
and was teeming with tropical swamps,
horsetail forests towering above the water,

before its landmass traveled the oceans,
tectonic clockwork conveying its shores
to the Arctic amid drifting continents.

Caving to curiosity, we comb the beach,
turning up among damp and pebbled soil
to the tactile fascination of our fingertips
the bleached heel bone and vertebrae
of a hapless seal, the broken humerus
and ulna of perhaps a tern, the armor husk
of an isopod large enough to fill our palms—
remnants of spent life yet to be erased.

Here, at the outset of our month on Ellesmere
to retrace how fish equipped us for footsteps
by pioneering the vertebrate limb, we pore
over our finds, their presence on this shore
short-lived as if script on parchment ever
scraped clean by changing latitudes and climate,
the island's older chapters effaced with death
and the birth of new species, habitats anciently
vanished into the ground we now stand on,
their traces left behind as fossils made legible
with the blade of a shovel and a drizzle of glue.

North of the Treeline

Warded off by prospects of frozen sap,
permafrost too hard for delving roots,
trees have found no ground on Ellesmere,
their absence as eerie as the emptiness
of a ghost town—From my vantage along
the slope, one would expect to see
the valley's immensity inhabited by stands
of bark-covered boles, the familiar sight
of treetop foliage tremulous in the wind.
Instead, without a single leaf to occlude
their view, I see our encampment's nine
tents dotting the length of vacant moss,
miniscule in a bend of the stream's thread.

Hiking on farther across the desolation,
finding only plant life at best able to greet
my ankles instills in me a longing for boughs
as missing wood draws out an overdue
realization that forking limbs are more
than perches for birds or green splashes
to offset concrete's gray, their wonders
only now valued within my recollection:

chloroplasts transmuting sunlight into sugar,
thirsty anchors rooting trunks in the earth,
chlorophyll jeweling canopies with emeralds
before dwindling for an autumnal shedding
of reds and ochers, umbers and oranges,
as malachite needles withstand snow's touch—

Images of tree rings and xylem waterways
that spring to mind from textbooks jumble
with a lifetime of skyward branches seen

in landscaped parks, along sidewalks
and interstates, and above the shade found
in my childhood's schoolyards to produce
a captivating forest, its intricate verdure
deserving better than fleeting interest.

Like left-behind stumps evoking felled trees,
the lack of woodland offers a fertile nostalgia:
coming here and sowing lessons and memories
long unrecalled in the island's fallow vistas,
an appreciation sprouts out of the tundra,
a seedling I hope to take south of the treeline
and rear to twine about unnoticed trunks,
a transplant among the backdropping green.

Ellesmere Elegy

This land dreams up marvels:

a meteorite shower of clumpy
snow streaking under midnight's sun.

This land embodies ruses:

broad valley floors and nondescript
slopes distorting scale and distance.

This land stages parables:

a lone caribou, its coat the color
of fog, curiously approaching humans.

This land emanates awe:

after a storm, the sun blasting its rays
through the sargassum of silvered clouds.

This land divulges ghosts:

among outcrops, the bones of dead life
forms weathering out from solidified silt.

This land inks its own elegy:

the ruin of a glacier on the horizon
hemorrhaging meltwater past our feet.

Gilled Beginnings

On the trail of oblivion's beasts,
their lives now nothing more
than tales sealed down in deposits
of bones sown epochs ago,
we have traveled across the globe
to search for their fabled remains
at this glacier-scraped latitude,
the lengths ventured to retrieve
their stories like something out of
the myth of seafarers after the gold
of a ram's flayed fleece, its wool
lying at the world's known edge
lustrous as a hearth's flame—

Leaving camp each morning,
trudging over dips and tussocks
of moss and following the treeless
valley, we come to the outcrop,
set about the sweat-beading business
of shoveling away overburden,
combing the hillside's scree
for the telltale hue and texture
betraying weathered-out bone,
scrappy inklings leading us
to where in the quarry we'll settle
on our knees, our focus trained
on the revelations of broken strata.

Working with awl and brush,
we clear away stone and dust, keen
to see what the rock will reward us
for having journeyed so far north—
Ancient sediment now cemented

crumbling before our tools, we expose
a placoderm's skull-roof armor
and the crushing teeth of lungfish
once the bane of snails and bivalves:
their bone bed marked with glyphs
of scattered fin rays records a scene
surviving an ecosystem vanished,
Devonian waters in its day
drowning where we now toil.

Exhuming this extinct shoal from
its stranding in the subterranean,
we whittle down the unknowns
that still riddle evolution's selection
of a fish to fashion into an amphibian,
this in turn starting a saga in which
amphibians were fashioned into reptiles,
and then reptiles into mammals,
with niches novel, vacated, or usurped
engraving their ossified signature
upon jaws, vertebrae, and limb bones,
braincases and encaging ribs
in workshops of mountains and deeps,
dunes and caves, jungles and rivers,
only at some point to stumble on
bipedal apes in a Miocene paradise,
dew-jeweled grasses and riverbanks
loud with purl song the testing
grounds for our upright strides—
millions of years of shape-shifting
since that first departure from water
leaving gilled beginnings forgotten to us.

Beneath the sun's ceaseless glare,
our jackets stripped off and cast aside,

we hunch over crack-hammered stone,
shoulders and arms sore from days
of toiling to piece together
the fractured lore of creations
glacially improvised, these bones
cached in strata our translator's key
to read lost tales in the language
of dead species: the origin
stories inscribed into skeletons
forever handed down and adapted,
vessels of rock-kept knowledge
embodying an anatomical chronicle
no less miraculous than
golden wool gleaming red.

Forlorn Fishermen

Falling sheets now drown this valley,
against which we can do nothing but
escape the deluge by confining ourselves
to our tents, the deafening patter shutting us in
like the stone surrounding buried fossils.

❧

Shovels and chisels lying abandoned
to a downpour, wooden handles sodden
in the quarry: a hope, already two days old,
waits with us warm and dry in our tents,
anxious for when the heavens exhaust
all their torrent and drizzle to resume
the pursuit of petrified fish, impatient with
the sun-shrouding gray still dousing us.

❧

Tents relocated after today's soaking lesson—
With the stream brimming over its banks,
rain-swollen waters reached into tents too
near the cresting current, proving the folly
of having eddy murmur within earshot to slumber,
the creeping rivulets licking sleepers awake.

❧

The sight of the quarry during droplets' lapse:
a small pond sits down at its center—Normally
a salvation to a fish stranded out of water,
this godsend comes epochs too late to avail gills here,
fins long too stony to find again their flutter.

Water scooped and hurled splashes the hillside
as we use plastic bottles to bail out the quarry
until heavy raindrops start to pelt our faces—
Jackets drying after retreating squelch-stepped
across mud and moss, we sit in our tents forlorn
like fishermen at a loss to face mere water.

The Charcoal Speck

After the last days' mists and rain,
the North's spectacle lures me
outside my tent's unzipped door:

the untrammeled blue effulgence
of a summer midnight ignorant
of moonlight and constellations,

July's omnipresent sun having banished
black, glistered skies to September,
well after we'll have returned south.

Overcome by a light breeze traveling
the valley, the oversized mosquitoes
find their ponderous swarms grounded,

emboldening me to wander farther
off from my tent's yellow to survey
the daylight insomnia of the tundra's

stubble of poppies, moss, and grass,
its stream restless among orange lichens.
With the others sleeping, sensible

victims of watch hands and circadian
fatigue, I have the valley to myself,
enjoying the crisp air stroking the hairs

along my bare arms, my jacket shed
to savor the sun's warm favor.
Walking to the water running camp side,

I kneel and cup the current inviting
to my increasingly shaggy face, revel in
the glacial chill passing down my throat.

Looking across to the far slope, I catch
a charcoal speck spying upon me
from a blind of hillocks and hollows—

a fox furtive in its seasonal color.
I suppose it's been eyeing all this while
the ease with which I've helped myself

to the stream and basked openly out in
the unsetting sun, as clueless as a kit
venturing for the first time out of its den.

Having seen enough, the fox abruptly
turns tail to follow a footpath wending
among moss knolls—its offward

slinking form like a brusque reproach
of my presuming for even a second
that I had this valley to myself.

Our Gilled Forebear

On uncovering a specimen of Tiktaalik roseae

Your time capsule broken open,
we breathe in the Devonian, taste
on our tongues the dust stirred up
from the siltstone relief you've become:
a jaw's wreckage, the brittle shroud
of scales overlying ribs, your retrofitted
fins and their newly crafted wrists, all
that once glided through shallows now
stone, like some unfortunate victim
happening to glance upon a gorgon.
Before continuing to rob you
from your grave, we stay our chisels—
Moments like this, I imagine,
should be akin to setting foot inside
a queen's hoard-filled sepulchre
or finding a monument's ruins
hidden away amidst jungled cliffs,
lost epics depicted on its friezes
crumbled by the grip of tree roots.
Yet in restoring you to sunlight,
I also feel a touch of the angler's rush
of the submerged pull, the bowed rod
and taut line, wavelet waters broken
by sun-silvered scales writhing in air,
our eyes captivated by the anatomy
crowning you as our ancestral chimera,
ancient amalgam of land and water.
Our gilled forebear, long slumbering
in the safety of your stratum, know
that the legacy unfolded from your wrists
today dares the clouds as an owl's wings,

tunnels through soil as a mole's paws,
sculls among reefs as a turtle's flippers,
your subsequent dynasty even finding
among its glory of fur, scales, and feathers
my own hand's thumb and four fingers
clutching a tool to release you from rock.
With your heirloom nubbins of bone
that braced your fins on streamside mud,
you bestowed to your descendants
the sky, the earth, and all the oceans,
as if some primordial and doting
parent that had wished for its children
lives redefining what can even be
imagined, giving them and the branching
lines of their progeny possibilities
ever evolving, whole worlds beyond
the reach of a fish, realms entered
just by stepping out of the water.

Muskox Memory

After more than two weeks,
our eyes have grown accustomed
to the tundra's sprawling amnesia
of trunk and bough, yet earlier this
morning, we encountered a muskox
become a memory succumbing
to moss, meat hook horns escaping
their skull's green overgrowth.
We stopped to inspect the twin
curves of keratin, lingering and last
traces of a dead bovid's debris, no
other bones visible among the green.
At month's end, shortly after we return
south, the signs of our presence here
will begin to fade, much like the tracks
of unseen caribou and polar bears
crumbling in dried mud. Among these vales,
where for days we've seen nothing stir,
the Earth premonishes disappearance,
the rote perishing disposing of the likes
of trilobites and moas, ammonites
and pterosaurs, tree-tall horsetails
and mastodons, four-toed horses
and triceratopses, their saga of loss
unfolding since prototype microbes
first fashioned life out of lifelessness—
Their passing lies beyond the horizon
of our memory, whole species gone
and forgotten by changing landscapes
save for stone's keepsakes: a handful
of skeletons, a shell's whorls,
pressed leaves, or ambered insects.
While the others resumed their way

to the day's digging, I lagged behind,
kneeling down in front of headstone horns,
my camera trained on a muskox's grave
to snap a photo before sheaths and cores
are erased from the moss, cracked
and moldered by years of freeze and thaw,
their vanishing just as inevitable as
the departure, hopefully some millennia
after I myself am buried, of shaggy herds
adapted to Ellesmere's unsparing wastes,
only a few remnant teeth or, perhaps,
a partial cranium left to attest deep
down out of mind in the Earth's strata
that their hooves once traveled these valleys,
the fog of their breath evaporated
into winter's night air like a figment.

Eggshell Future

Trekking among till stones
abandoned by retreating ice,
I glimpse down at my muddy boots
and think of yesterday, how
I stopped my foot in midair,
close to crashing it down
onto a scrape harboring four
eggs speckled over with brown,
the mother plover accosting me
in wingbeat panic, her rendition
of a broken wing both ploy and plea
to lure my human footsteps away
and safeguard an eggshell future.

The Past's Chronicler

For Farish

He points to a white smidge
atop a peak that nearly a month
before saddled the whole ridge:
Twenty years ago, that ice would
last the whole summer—Coming
to the Arctic from year to year,
you can see the Earth warming . . .

As I listen to him recount how
the summer melt has changed
over two decades, he makes plain
that his memory holds a record
of abundance predating our present
depauperate day: only yesterday
he told of first beholding herds
of elephants as a graduate student
out on the savannah, awe driving him
to carefully observe the prehensile
precision of their trunks plucking
leaves and pulling branches to mouth,
how they gently caressed one another
with those boneless lengths, a sight
that would become rarer and rarer
on his return trips to East Africa.

But in the sunny polar evenings
in the coziness of the kitchen tent,
sometimes his chronicles shift
to the beginnings of his sixty-six years—
A few days ago, after teaching me
how to cook a mushroom risotto

using previously shipped provisions—
the trick is to continuously stir
and let the grains absorb all the stock
before adding the next ladleful—
he began to regale us over dinner
with tales of teenage derring-do
and the countryside summers
of his boyhood, when he would join
his cousins in gunslinger games
mimicked from westerns—*the air*
thick with bullets—before launching
into the episode of the failed manhunt
to find the boys who badly beat one
of his cousins, which, in his hindsight,
luckily came down to empty-handed
hours spent walking back roads.

His trade, though, is not even
human memory—When in the quarry
with eyes cast down on his awl,
the fossils emerging as he scratches
inspire his words to reach back
whole epochs and eras to recap
events preceding our appearance.
One of his favorite subjects is how
from among a constellation of traits
the first mammals were minted—
Going beyond the obvious attributes
of warm blood, fur, and milk,
he tells how bones co-opted from
a reptilian jaw became our ear's
incus and malleus, how novel joints
allowed limbs to abandon a posture
with elbows held akimbo, how millstone
molars morphed out of occluding

tooth cusps, how together all these
innovations led to today's cohort
of hippos, squirrels, and wolves,
porpoises, opossums, and bats,
the myriad species that make up
Mammalia's evolved menagerie.

However, he can also just as easily
converse about his university,
where he and his colleagues delve
into the locomotion of live animals
by bringing them into the laboratory.
Ever the storyteller, he's not one
to limit our talk to gaits, treadmills,
muscle forces, or kinematics,
often digressing into the oddball
incidents that only arise in research.
While recalling how he once had
echidnas amble under an X-ray camera
to measure their skeletal movements
concealed inside pincushion hides,
he veered into his memory of the time
he had to cover on short notice
a physiology lecture, filling in
for another professor who suffered
an emergency only later explained
when that professor reappeared in
the department, his left eye bandaged
over with gauze sharing a lesson
learned through clawed protest: *never*
stick a thermometer up the rectum
of a fully conscious adult cheetah.

He finishes telling me of Arctic ice
and then pauses, taking in the valley.

Turning to me with a smile, he gestures
to the view before us, *Aren't we lucky
that we get to come here and see this?*,
his eyes glinting with our present story,
before it too is compiled with the past.

Dead Reverence

As we trench around what was once a fish,
skull shards, rhombus scales, and cleithra only
offering a gist of its past existence, I wonder how
the gilled community of its Devonian waters
would have viewed it perhaps patiently waiting
for the moment of ambush or maybe prowling
slowly with jaws slightly ajar among sunken
vegetation, my thoughts trying to resuscitate
a ruin of bones disarrayed in stone:

in the dapple of sunrays spearing murky eddies,
whereby flashes of gold infiltrated the gloom,
did all the streambed's fish—their schools boasting
plate armor skeletons, shell-crushing teeth,
sweep-thrust tails, and needle-thin fangs—recognize
that they were witnessing a watershed miracle
of aquatic evolution:

                         the flat triangular head,
the nostrils at the tip of its snout lifted clear
of the stream by a short neck, the eyes atop
the skull rising to skim their gaze across the surface,
before a long body reinforced by ribs and pushing
with wrists vanished out of water onto land?

Despite that moment's gravity, when bones first
experimented with shoring up a body's weight
before flowering into mammals, birds, and reptiles,
those fish likely had not the slightest clue what
they were seeing—for who has time to muse
over marvels of anatomy when you're subject
to laws revolving around closing jaws, preoccupied
with filling your stomach with your next meal
while avoiding winding up in another's belly?

But since when has the compulsion to consume
ever abided wonder? It's not even as if I could claim
we humans are any better than those ancient fins
that stalked Devonian swamps: I doubt the poacher
stuffing a pangolin, scales tightly balled, into a sack
or a half-starved sailor harpooning a sea cow
would halt their hands to ponder the adaptive feats
embodied as keratin armor or Arctic gigantism—
just the same, I suspect, for the hunter that squeezed
the trigger to deliver a rhino to the museum's hall
of mammals, which, motionlessly outliving its lifetime,
cemented itself into my childhood's fascination.

Tending to this skeleton on this far northern
outcrop, jacketing its fragile form with layers
of moistened toilet paper followed by layers
of wet plaster, we unearth this fossil with a reverence
that I'd wager was alien to this fish when alive:
long without any flesh to devour or motions
to still, its ramshackle remains at last unlock,
like diorama fauna revived by our imagination,
the due awe never found while it was breathing.

Southern Constellations

Now in the closing days,
the quarry again stands silent,
our tools largely packed away
as the fossils recovered over
this past month now sit within
the kitchen tent, their jacketing
plaster ghostly in its shade—
With the expedition nearly over,
I take about an hour each evening
to venture off from the others,
seizing these final chances
and the absent risk of nightfall
to quest for wildflowers
among the tundra's hollows:
a souvenir from this land where
the summer sun never sets.
Bare fingertips burning
from the near-August cold,
I pluck stems of lemon-cup
poppies, collect white bells
of heather, stash delicate
globes of campion to press
between waterproof pages,
putting to use the field notebook
that I have neglected to fill with
my thoughts here on Ellesmere,
reflections on dwarf caribou,
the lost histories lived out
by fossil fish, and my fortune
not to happen upon a polar bear
all unrecorded but leaving room
instead to prepare this present.
Knowing that I will soon

again see dark eyes distant
in Chicago, hear your softly
Southern accent last heard
in a sidewalk goodbye,
I let my imagination indulge me
with the moment that petals
page-bound pass from my hands
into yours, when I rediscover
a sight outsized in its absence
despite the awe of finding
bone mementos of fallen
species and feeling the warmth
of a midnight sun grace my skin:
the constellations in the darkness
of your eyes after going thirty
days on this island at a loss
to behold the night and its stars.

A Blank Page

In these parting minutes, the sunlight
is lavish enough to give us a sky
passable for a polished blue gem
while we close our time on Ellesmere
readying ourselves for the Twin Otter
and a late morning return to Resolute,
the beds and hot showers awaiting us
now restful decadences after a month
of tents and sleeping bags, poor shaves,
and having only the gooseflesh option
to wash ourselves in the valley's stream.

After we've packed all our tools, camping
gear, and haul of fossils for departure,
I'm sure that the others' ears are alert
for the propeller drone announcing
the plane's imminent approach
as they mill about making small talk
or stoop down to shoot saxifrage petals,
fuchsia enlarged through a macro lens—
My footsteps, though, are called forth
to where waves test the toes of my water-
proof boots, a booming barely audible
drawing me by ear toward the offing.

I see nothing out in the sound's direction
save for cobalt eddies, leaving me
to suppose it could be the machinery
on a factory-sized ship winching aboard
colossal catches of fish or the handiwork
of fellow scientists mining novel data
from the depths; however, I would rather
imagine the clashing of floes and calving

icebergs quaking oceans, waters pitching
with mountain-high crests overpowering
even whole pods of whales—

Beached and lending credence to
my preferred explanation, a raft of ice
rests halfway in the wash some yards off,
melting contours all slick with sun glare,
somehow having lasted this late into July
though no other ice lies within sight,
its oblong length like a sailor collapsed
ashore after escaping maritime calamity.

Soon its thawing remainder will mingle
with the surf and rejoin Arctic currents,
and I suspect too that this booming—
whatever its source—will also come
to an end, with either leaving no trace
in accordance with the earthly law
of unending turnover that sweeps away
mountains and oceans just the same
as ice and echoes and every species
to have ever evolved over four billion
laps circling the sun, their lost stories
tantalizing us like a blank page that begs
us to guess what now stands unknown
in annals recorded in disappearing ink.

Carrion Knowledge

Long before our current constellation
of seven continents, the upthrust
of Andes and Rockies, the vibrant
calcium of the Great Barrier Reef;
interminably before our handiwork
of concrete and ink, pasture and war,
the mote glories of pyramids and Angkor,
there was the root of this knowledge:

a dead fish,

its eyes filmed over, the carcass half-
eaten before the opportune burial
by the sludge of primordial
floodwaters, the skeleton flesh bereft
in a future desolation of outcrops,
its bones beckoning the final scavengers,
enticing us to pick them clean, down
to the last scraps of carrion knowledge.

IV. BLINDFOLD WONDER

The Oceanographer

Inspired by the Carta Marina *of Olaus Magnus*

I know the swirls and eddies of these seas
like the lines navigating my own palms.
I have traveled the seas to all the world's
corners—spice harbors beyond the map's
borders, merchant ports brimming with ducats,
the rock face caves of runners and smugglers.
My time on these waves has wizened my brow,
while the salt winds have gnawed my hair brittle
and lashed knuckles clenched round my raised spyglass.

Like your irises' rivaling sapphire,
blue waves shield what impels and inhabits.

Yet for all my share of amassed nicks and wears,
the sea has ever bloomed marvels before me—
floating jellies harried by hull-backed turtles,
seahorses tail-twined in kelp-waft gardens,
octopus caretaking crab-shell graveyards,
frost-seals swooping amongst berg-sunk shipwrecks,
spires of towering reef cities flourished
in reds and ochers, emerald and silver,
ringed in trains of sharks, eels, and gem-scaled fish.

All their splendor hidden deep in sapphire,
dark hues stolen from your lambent blue eyes.

I steel myself for seawater frontiers,
my compass bent upon the horizon's
blue gilt, guiding me in dugout and skiff,
agile longship and high-walled galleon.
I welcome the sun's scorch to batter cracked skin,

I savor spume's kiss upon my dry lips,
I hail the boom of colliding ice floes.
Let the crash of waves hurl me to seas undiscerned,
and douse-blinding storms test my mariner's wits.

All my daring to dull haunting sapphire,
old seines ensnaring through your rippling blue.

Beneath capricious sprawls of jostling waves
lurk beasts fathomless in their sunless lairs
beguiling by siren song in briny swells.
There is no gold too dear to know what sits
and speeds amongst dark-gulfed trenches and vales,
breaching to sun's gaze from peregrine deeps
from Faroe south to Arctic deserts north—
wonders refuged in sunken hinterlands,
luring my eyes to domains foiling light.

All their strangeness masked by your rich sapphire,
though I fled your veiling blue so long ago.

Where heavens join ocean in seam of night
stalk mysteries beneath prows towing dawn—
kraken slaughtering by the maelstrom's gyre,
whale-fish breathing geysers to flip frail rafts,
vast serpents splintering ships in vise coils,
mermaids and gorgons rescuing sailors
thrown overboard in maritime tempests,
hauling them abreast porpoises to white shores,
nursing them on fruits plucked from seafloor groves.

All dwellers ensconced in unplumbed sapphire,
like your thoughts stirring below lidded blue.

Tireless, I sound each groundswell's dark-homed root,
salvaging crude inklings of seabed-born
riddles mirrored in spindrift irises.
Line in hand, I know the sea will outlast
my vigil long between terror and awe,
bringing me solace and slumber final
at foundations of currents and abyss,
where among formless ruins a net-shawled goddess
strokes the brows of drowned sailors and lovers.

Resting where flickered shadows billow sapphire,
serene among darkness birthing your blue.

Blindfold Wonder

In the mammal skeleton collections of the Museum für
Naturkunde Berlin

I suppose that if Dr. Morton had met me,
he would have fantasized about my skull
assuming its place among the shelves
of his collection, yet here, among these
wood-and-glass cabinets safeguarding walrus
tusks, zebra skull grins, and platypus bills,
I would like to think that with the dead
I have found my place. In the ossuary quiet,
the braying, roaring, bellowing long silenced,
though I train my eyes on an aardvark's humerus
as my calipers' blades capture its length,
the brown skin of my fingers nonetheless glares
against the bone's cortical whiteness.

After entering its length into a spreadsheet, I return
the humerus to its skeleton's cardboard box,
next fishing out a femur—As I glide the calipers
along its shaft, I try again to rebind my eyes
with the blindfold wonder now threadbare
since the days it swaddled my childhood gaze:

I remember when I was four years old, the yellow
of taxis on the George Washington Bridge,
the white marble of the museum's facade,
a timeline recorded in a giant sequoia's tree rings,
a giant squid plucked from the aphotic abyss,
a blue whale as massive as an ocean god incarnate,
the wild dogs gazing into the Serengeti sunset.
Most of all I remember the toothy height
of the *Tyrannosaurus* towering tiny armed

over my family and other museum visitors,
flanked on its left by its foe *Triceratops*
brandishing horns and a frill: the menagerie
of my coloring books escaped from their pages
to steer my life's course to these bones in Berlin—
That first pilgrimage capped with hot dogs
in the museum's food court while I beamed over
a toy *T. rex* molded from burgundy plastic.

Returning to New York two decades later, no longer
prone to my boyhood's unseeing wonder,
I could read the symbols in the bronze sight
of Roosevelt greeting me at the museum's entrance,
his horseback height cementing his head far above
the paired African and American natives attending
him on foot: the tarnished trio standard-bearers
for the halls within, where under the umbrella
of the uncivilized world, dark peoples deemed
inferior and doomed to the fate of Tasmanian tigers,
dodos, and great auks find themselves
relegated to the ranks of eagles and moose,
bongos and gorillas, and a centerpiece herd
of African elephants, their cultures whittled
down to whelk-shell costumes and carved tusks,
beast-stacking totems and raven-faced masks,
while among exhibits' periphery the ghost
of a museum director, once a champion of fossils
and eugenics, grimaced at my footsteps.

That was 2007. Now in Berlin, in this foreign city
become my home, I skirt the atrocities concealed
behind species christened out of Greek and Latin
—*Orycteropus, Proteles, Trichechus, Phataginus*—
their naming authors advancing after colonizing
bayonets into the voids carved out by genocides,

their soles wiped clean of gunpowder and blood
underfoot by the pursuit of romanticized discovery,
hypotheses peerless on an alabaster pedestal.
Working in the light of the mezzanine's window,
recording the lengths of the radius and ulna,
I sit in a shadow cast amid fanfare in 1937,
when down below in the museum's grand atrium,
the *Brachiosaurus* was unveiled to cameras flashing
upwards beneath its neck snaking to the ceiling,
a backdrop of swastikas blazoning the walls.

Other shadows inhabit emptied eye sockets,
recede into marrow cavities and vertebral crannies
to weather the curated forgetting—
Buried in the facelessness of our silence,
black omissions whisper from graves left unmarked,
insistent on restoring life to their decayed memory:
the shoulders that ported crates of specimens,
the lips that shared knowledge of roots and herbs,
birds and beasts, terrain and geography,
the hands that cleared paths and quarries
all resurface to undermine the blue-eyed fantasy
that the Earth was a naturalist's birthright to tame.

Taking the tibia in one hand, the calipers' gape I adjust
with the other, my fingers' exactitude unwavering,
as if hands like my own were never excluded
from this graveyard ordered into aisles, never denied
the nets and rifles that filled these shelves, never barred
from microscopes and scalpels, never banned
from learning housed in archives and libraries;
as if our manifold browns were never condemned
to a background invisibility, its trappings
of brooms pushed down hallways, flashlights to patrol
after hours, the ladles serving museum visitors.

Though not invisible, I remain a rarity, and—as any
trophy hunter could tell you—rarity all too often merits
a target upon your hide, as when a revered graybeard
takes aim with his seminar topic—*Black people
are not as smart as White people*—his erudite racism
challenged by averted eyes and silence, just as when
among attic antlers, a curator makes time to shoot
her question—*Who are you, and what do you think
you're doing?*—blind to your dangling visitor's badge,
or when, in your head, out creeps the voice
of a craniologist hunting in the nineteenth century—
*Whom could I perhaps pay now, so I can collect
his skull and measure its volume after his death?*—
Despite the shelter found in deadening your retinas,
steadfast wonder does little to deafen your ears.

Finished with the fibula, I rest its slender length
with the other bones in its cardboard coffin before
I turn to the next boxed aardvark, rifling around
to pluck out a humerus. To wholly marvel again
at its aardvark biology—the thirty-centimeter tongue,
its dentine teeth missing enamel, nocturnal
secrecy and its subsistence on termites, ants,
and the occasional cucumber, the fact that it lingers
on after thirty million years of evolution
as the last survivor of its lineage—I try to re-cinch
the awe once inuring my eyes, with its tatters pretend
that these bones of this misfit among mammals
were always intended to pass into my hands.

NOTES

Natural History, the Curious Institution—From the fifteenth to the eighteenth century, naturalists in Europe relied upon ships traveling across the Atlantic to bring, if not additionally source and collect, specimens from Africa and the Americas. One of the larger components of transatlantic sea traffic was slave ships bringing enslaved people from Africa to the New World, and in turn bringing goods and materials, either in small or large quantities, back to Europe—the so-called triangular trade. From surviving records and correspondence, we know that the English naturalists James Petiver and Hans Sloane greatly relied on the slave trade to acquire new specimens. Though records have not survived for other European naturalists, it seems unlikely that only these two naturalists would have co-opted the slave trade for their benefit.

The choice to include a given species or organism in the poem was based primarily on when a species received its binomial name. If a species received its name prior to 1808, the year the transatlantic slave trade ended, it means that the species was known to naturalists formally, and before that anecdotally, before the end of the slave trade. Species native to West Africa and the Americas are included, as a single slave ship could have brought specimens back from both geographic regions.

The voices found in the poem are not found texts but are instead based upon the documented realities of the slave trade and historical events, such as the wreck of the *São José-Paquete de Africa* (stanza 9) and the *Zong* massacre (stanza 25). The line *"the iron savored our blood and entered our souls"* (in stanza 19) quotes an enslaved man named

Caesar, whose story is told in John Riland's 1827 novel *Memoirs of a West-India Planter*.

The opening quote from Kathleen Murphy is from *The William and Mary Quarterly* vol. 70, no. 4 (October 2013).

Dioramic Idylls—A *chicotte* is a whip made of dried rhinoceros or hippopotamus hide.

Rhinoceros Relic—The Sumatran rhinoceros diorama at the Copenhagen Zoological Museum was dismantled in 2023, after the museum's closure. The population numbers in the opening note come from the International Union for Conservation of Nature's Red List of Threatened Species. As bad as the outlook is for the Sumatran rhinoceros, the situation is even bleaker for its relative the Javan rhinoceros (*Rhinoceros sondaicus*).

The Last Sea Cow's Testimony—The behaviors of the sea cow as well as the imagery and details of how it was hunted are based upon Georg Wilhelm Steller's 1751 volume *De bestiis marinis* (*The Beasts of the Sea*).

Lettow-Vorbeck and His Uncatchable Lizard—Although Lettow-Vorbeck was considered a hero in Germany for resisting a force of 300,000 Allied soldiers with only 14,000 soldiers during World War I's East Africa campaign (1914–1918), he also caused a regional famine that killed as many as 350,000 Africans by conscripting food and men from the indigenous population. Collected in German East Africa (today Tanzania) from 1909 to 1913, *Dysalotosaurus lettowvorbecki* was not named until 1920. Coined by the paleontologist Josef Pompeckj, the genus name *Dysalotosaurus* is derived by combining the Greek words *dysálōtos* ("difficult to catch") and *saúros* ("lizard").

Memory Museum—*Mein Vater Erklärt Mir Jeden Sonntag Unsere Neun Planeten* is a mnemonic device to recall the names of the nine planets of the solar system (when Pluto was counted among them). "Bang" in line 30 refers to the Big Bang.

Noriko—*Donburi* is a Japanese dish consisting of fish, meat, or vegetables served over rice, and *negi* are Japanese scallions. *Sakana* is the Japanese word for "fish."

Frau Kahnt—*U-Boot, Bomben,* and *Mutter* are German for "submarine," "bombs," and "mother," respectively. The line *"Mein Mann ist tot seit acht Jahren"* translates to "my husband has been dead for eight years."

Otepää Snowscape—*Vangla* means "prison." *Vasakale* and *paremale* mean "to the left" and "to the right," respectively. *Sini-must-valge* ("blue-black-white") is a colloquialism for the Estonian flag. The town of Otepää is popularly known as Estonia's "winter capital."

It Came from Beneath the Sea—*Cavaquinha* is the Brazilian Portuguese term for the Brazilian slipper lobster (*Scyllarides brasiliensis*).

Moqueca **Chronicle**—*Moqueca* is a Brazilian stew typically made with fish. Unlike the versions from the states of Espírito Santo and Pará, the version from the state of Bahia is distinct in using *dendê* oil and coconut milk, which attest to an African influence. In his 2007 book *The Slave Ship: A Human History*, Marcus Rediker tells that a dish called "dab-a-dab" was fed to enslaved Africans during the Middle Passage. "Crews" were small bowls in which the dab-a-dab was served. The "cat's scars" is a reference to the cat-o'-nine-tails, and *senzala* is the Portuguese term for slave quarters. The actual recipe featured in the poem is based upon Thiago Castanho's recipe in the 2014 book he co-authored with Luciana Bianca, *Brazilian Food*.

Erinnerung—*Erinnerung* is the German word for "memory," and the lines *"die andere, wo der Vater / herrisch und kontrollsüchtig ist"* translate to "the other where the father / is domineering and control seeking."

Dispatches from Ellesmere—Today, the pelvic fin/hindlimb anatomy of *Tiktaalik* is also largely, but not wholly, known based upon fossils recovered during the 2006 expedition to Ellesmere Island (with a description being published in 2014). As this anatomy was not known during the course of the 2006 expedition upon which the poem is based, I did not consider making references to *Tiktaalik*'s pelvic fin/hindlimb anatomy in the poems, keeping a focus on the animal's pectoral fin/forelimb.

ACKNOWLEDGMENTS

Several of the poems in this collection first appeared in literary magazines and journals which gave me my first opportunities to publicly share my work and, through rejection, persistence, and success, taught me the basics of literary publishing. I warmly express my thanks to the following for publishing the respective poems:

Artemis: Orison
Catamaran Literary Reader: Dioramic Idylls
The Common: Ellesmere Elegy; A Blank Page
Decolonial Passage: The Giraffe Titan (II)
Ecotone: Natural History, the Curious Institution
The Fourth River: Boyhood's Fields
The Hopper: Rhinoceros Relic
Jabberwock Review: Noriko; The Charcoal Speck
Obsidian: Blindfold Wonder
The Offing: Lettow-Vorbeck and His Uncatchable Lizard; The Location
    We Look For
Panel: Otepää Snowscape
Poet Lore: The Giraffe Titan (I)
Santa Fe Literary Review: Frau Kahnt; Creation Myth
Sea to Sky Review: The Oceanographer
SLANT: The Origami Fox
Split Rock Review: The Last Sea Cow's Testimony; Muskox Memory
Tahoma Literary Review: Memory Museum
Terrain.org: Our Gilled Forebear
West Trade Review: *Moqueca* Chronicle; *Erinnerung*

I also would like to thank Pille-Riin Larm and *Sirp* for publishing a translation, by Peeter Sauter, of "Otepää Snowscape," which gave me the opportunity to share a small piece of my work with an Estonian audience.

For encouraging my interest in poetry early on, I can only express my gratitude toward Laurie Godshall, Diane Touchet, Melinda Mangham, Bobette Castille, and Donna Krippse. Many friends and colleagues also encouraged the pursuit of my craft, whether by giving me enthusiastic words and feedback or attending a reading, leaving me thankful for the kindness of Donna Stonecipher, Sianne Ngai, David M. Halperin, Mark McGurl, Reinhart Meyer-Kalkus, Sara Abbas, Josh Ostergaard, Yessica Klein, Stan Spring, Kim Kean, Yara Haridy, Róisín Tangney, Brian Crawford, Nicola Caroli, Tessa Scott, Francesca Bianco, Alexandra Connerty, Winifred Wong, Katarina Gotic, Gretchen Young, Subhashini Kaligotla, Maurice Carlos Ruffin, Jan Verberkmoes, Arianna Sullivan, Alexey Evstratov, Johan Renaudie, Antoine Verriere, Merlin Jansen, Gisela Günther, Karolina Radoń, Ella Koch, Eva Bendel, Marybeth Lima, Carla Reimold, Tiit Maran, Carla Scheunemann, Andrea Lukova, Joshua Miller, Christiane Funk, Peter Makovicky, Akiko Shinya, Nadia Fröbisch, Claire Dawkins, Milla Sumelius, Nathan Smith, Anika Chouaya, Ermin Grbo, and Alexander Kayales. For their encouragement to explore the legacies of slavery and colonialism within natural history, I also thank members of TheMuseumsLab and the Humanities of Nature: Anita Hermannstädter, Meryem Korun, Vivien Kreft, Celina Mützel, Solveig Rietschel, Susan Kamel, Gregor Schuster, Tahani Nadim, Ina Heumann, Catarina Madruga, and Katja Kaiser. There are also numerous colleagues who helped me to think about how poetry and science can come together, and for these discussions and their encouragement, I warmly acknowledge John Nyakatura, Sushma Reddy, John Holmes, Isabel Galleymore, Constanze Bickelmann, Sarah Werning, Sandra Sarr, Oliver Garden, Prosanta Chakrabarty, Chris Barrett, John Barnie, Jessica Ware, Kyla Beguesse, and Johannes Müller.

I thank my parents Jacquelyn and Donald Kilbourne for instilling in me a love for books and reading, and I thank them and my sister

Christa Kilbourne, as well as aunts and uncles Valerie Colson, Regina Escher, Alva Franklin, and Rehana and Greg Bates, as well as the rest of my family, for their support, enthusiasm, and encouragement. I also thank my parents, as well as my aunts and uncles Gwen and Edgar Ramsey and Darlene and Marvin Anthony, for that first trip to the American Museum of Natural History those many, many years ago and all it set in motion.

For giving me a platform to share my work, I thank Black in Natural History Museums and JC Buckner and Adania Flemming in particular. I also thank Gurmeet Singh and Siddhartha Lokanandi for the chance to read at Hopscotch Reading Room and Kristi Daniel for the chance to read at Jää-äär. I am grateful to Jessica Ware for the invitation to read at the 2022 Joint Annual Meeting of the Entomological Society of America, the Entomological Society of Canada, and the Entomological Society of British Columbia; John Holmes for the invitation to read at the Oxford University Museum of Natural History for the 2022 Symbiosis conference; Matt Friedman and Selena Smith for the invitation to read at the University of Michigan for the 2024 North American Paleontological Convention; Peter Makovicky, David Fox, Sushma Reddy, and Holly Menninger for an invitation to give a poetry reading at the Bell Museum as the public lecture for the 2024 Society of Vertebrate Paleontology Annual Meeting; and Marianthi Ioannidis and Kyla Beguesse for the invitation to read as part of the Off Country program of the Wildlife Disease Association's 2024 Annual Conference.

For awarding me the Cave Canem Prize and this chance to share my work, my immense gratitude goes to Dante Micheaux, the Cave Canem Foundation, and the contest judge Natasha Trethewey. I also thank the staff of Graywolf Press for bringing *Natural History* to the world, in particular Jeff Shotts for polishing my work with his years of experience in editing poems, as well as Brittany Torres Rivera and Katie Dublinski for further edits and polishing. For the cover design, I thank Mary Austin Speaker, and for my author photo, I thank Jamila K. Grote. For the book design, I thank Rachel Holscher.

Although I had no clue that I would write poems about Ellesmere Island back in 2006, I also thank Neil Shubin, Ted Daeschler, and Farish Jenkins for the opportunity to travel to the Arctic and participate in fieldwork. That field season has paid off in ways that I then could never have dreamed.

Travel has turned out to be an integral part of my writing process, and I am indebted to the cities of Budapest, Tallinn, Prague, Vienna, Nairobi, Barcelona, Helsinki, São Paulo, Santiago, Harare, Cape Town, Tbilisi, Copenhagen, Zagreb, Cork, and Stockholm. Being in these cities and discovering, or in some cases rediscovering, their character helped shape these poems, even if it was simply a matter of clearing my head to deliberately think and (re)consider my writing. I would also be remiss in not acknowledging Jena for offering the necessary bit of isolation (this is meant as a compliment) to initially focus on developing my craft and Berlin, in particular the Wissenschaftskolleg zu Berlin, for offering me my first experiences in engaging with other poets as well as with literary scholars.

This book is dedicated to Emma Greig, whose enthusiasm for my poetry was second to none. Despite her being—in her own estimation—no expert in poetry, I am grateful for the time she took to read my work and for her feedback over the years, and I'll always appreciate that she never faltered to congratulate me on my successes, even when her health was rapidly deteriorating. Though she was not able to see this book appear, the words found in its pages are an embodiment of her encouragement.

BRANDON KILBOURNE is an evolutionary biologist, having earned his BS in biological engineering at Louisiana State University and his PhD in evolutionary biology at the University of Chicago. He is a Cave Canem Fellow and was a College for Life Sciences Fellow of the Berlin Institute for Advanced Study. He was also artist-in-residence in the School of Veterinary Medicine at Louisiana State University. Kilbourne's poems have appeared in *The Common, Ecotone, Obsidian, Poet Lore, Tahoma Literary Review,* and *Terrain.org,* among other publications, and he has given readings at conferences on entomology, natural history, and paleontology in the United States, the United Kingdom, and Canada. A research biologist with over twenty years of experience, he has worked at the Denver Museum of Nature & Science, the Field Museum of Natural History, and the Museum für Naturkunde Berlin, as well as with collections from across the globe. He is a curatorial member of TheMuseumsLab, a joint learning program bringing together museum and heritage professionals from Africa and Europe for discussions on colonial legacies, restitution, and equity.

Graywolf Press publishes risk-taking, visionary writers who transform culture through literature. As a nonprofit organization, Graywolf relies on the generous support of its donors to bring books like this one into the world.

This publication is made possible, in part, by the voters of Minnesota through a Minnesota State Arts Board Operating Support grant, thanks to a legislative appropriation from the arts and cultural heritage fund. Significant support has also been provided by other generous contributions from foundations, corporations, and individuals. To these supporters we offer our heartfelt thanks.

To learn more about Graywolf's books
and authors or make a tax-deductible donation,
please visit www.graywolfpress.org.

The text of *Natural History* is set in Adobe Jenson Pro.
Book design by Rachel Holscher.
Composition by Bookmobile Design & Digital
Publisher Services, Minneapolis, Minnesota.
Manufactured by Versa Press on acid-free,
30 percent postconsumer wastepaper.